STARCHY FOODS

FOODS

HEALTHY EATING

BY GEMMA McMULLEN

CONTENTS

©2016
Book Life
King's Lynn
Norfolk PE30 4LS

Written by:
Gemma McMullen
Edited by:
Grace Jones
Designed by:
Drue Rintoul & Ian McMullen

ISBN: 978-1-910512-42-5

A catalogue record for this book is available from the British Library.

Look out for the underlined words in this book, they are explained in the glossary on page 24.

WHAT ARE STARCHY FOODS?

Bread, pasta, potatoes and food made from grains are starchy foods.

Bread

Wheat

Pasta

Eating starchy foods gives our bodies energy and keeps them healthy.

Starchy foods contain carbohydrates

GRAINS

Grains are small, hard, dry seeds from plants. They are used to make our food. Oats, wheat and rice are grains.

Oats

Wheat

Rice

Some grains are ground into flour. Others, such as rice, need to be cooked. Breakfast cereals are made with grains.

Rice Grains

Cooked Rice

Porridge (Oats)

Cereal (Corn)

RICE

Rice grows well in hot climates. Most of the world's rice is grown in Asia.

Rice

Many farmers use special fields called paddy fields to grow rice. These fields are in wet areas.

A Paddy Field

WHEAT

Wheat seeds are planted in the late autumn. Wheat needs plenty of rain to grow.

Wheat is harvested in the summer using a combine harvester.

BREAD

The main ingredient in bread is flour. Flour is a fine powder made from <u>grinding</u> cereal grains. It is most commonly made from wheat.

Wheat Grain

Flour

Bread comes in many forms and can be both savoury and sweet. Bread can be eaten for breakfast, lunch or dinner.

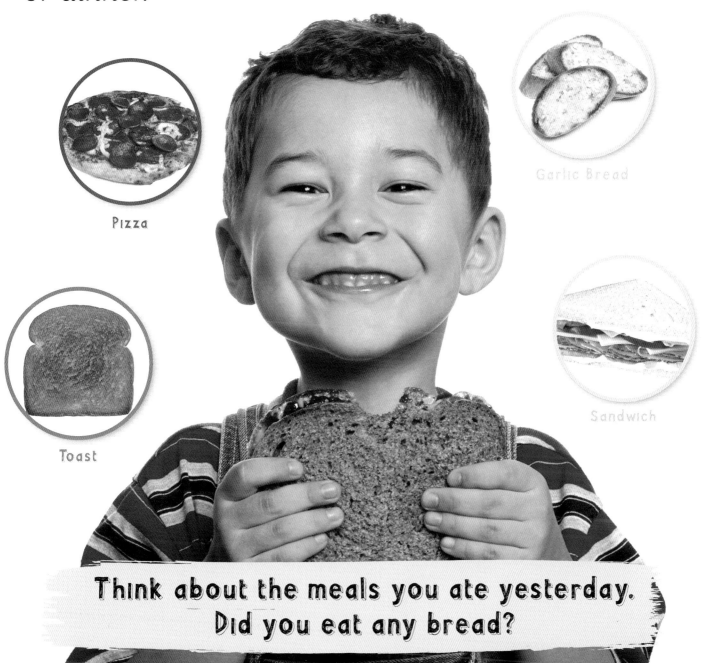

Pizza

Garlic Bread

Toast

Sandwich

Think about the meals you ate yesterday. Did you eat any bread?

13

PASTA

Like bread, the main ingredient in pasta is usually wheat flour. Pasta traditionally comes from Italy, but it is widely used in the UK too.

ITALY

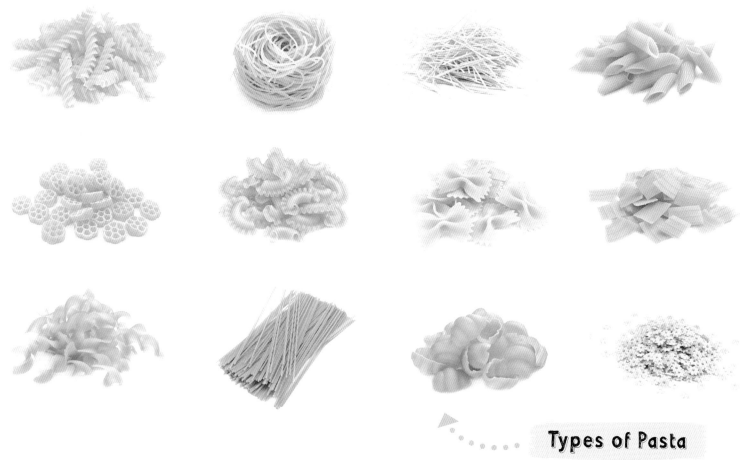

Types of Pasta

Pasta is used in savoury dishes, such as lasagne and spaghetti bolognese.

Pasta can be enjoyed warm or cold.

Lasagne

15

POTATOES

The potato is a root vegetable, but is classed as a starchy food alongside rice and pasta.

Potatoes can be used as part of any main meal.
They can be boiled, baked or fried.

Sausages and
Mashed Potatoes

Burger and Chips

Roast Potatoes

Chicken and
Boiled Potatoes

Jacket Potato with Cheese

17

HEALTHY STARCH

Starchy foods are carbohydrates that give our bodies energy. Starchy food should be a part of all our meals.

Sometimes, only part of the grain is used to make foods. The healthiest starchy foods are made by using the whole grain.

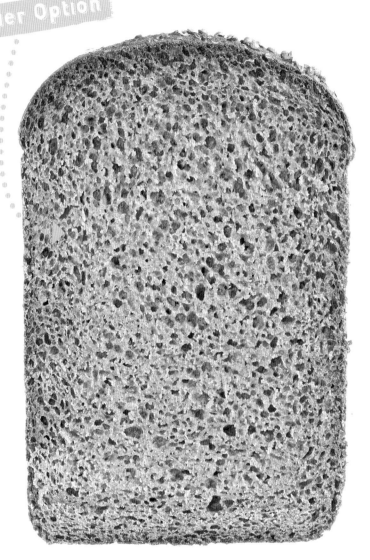

Healthier Option

White Bread
(Part of the Grain)

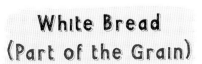

Brown Bread
(Whole Grain)

Some starchy foods are not as good as others for our bodies. This is because ingredients such as sugar and fat have been added to them.

It is fine to eat these foods in small amounts.

Doughnuts

Biscuits

Muffins

Pie

21

BREAD FROM AROUND THE WORLD

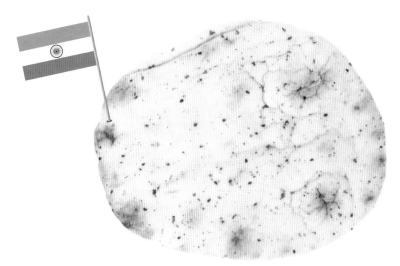

Naan bread comes from India. It is a flat bread enjoyed all over Southeast Asia.

Ciabatta bread is an Italian white bread made with flour and olive oil.

A baguette is a long, thin loaf of bread from France.

A pretzel is a German bread which is usually shaped like a knot.

GLOSSARY

carbohydrates
food that contains sugar and starch which gived us energy

climate
the typical weather of a certain area

combine harvester
a large machine which collects grain

grinding
to crush into small parts

root vegetable
a vegetable which comes from the root of a plant

INDEX

PHOTO CREDITS

Photocredits: Abbreviations: l-left, r-right, b-bottom, t-top, c-centre, m-middle. All images are courtesy of Shutterstock.com.

1 - Nattika. 2 - Valentyn Volkov. 3t - Melica. 3b - Elena Schweitzer. 4mr – Timmary. 4ml – Julia Ivantsova. 4b – JeniFoto. 5 – Noam Armonn. 6 – Vladimir Melnik. 6l, 10 – Igor Strukov. 6b – Javier Crespo. 6r – themorningglory. 7bl – MaraZe. 7br – Oliver Hoffmann. 7m – Freer. 7tr - zkruger. 8 – Andrii Gorulko. 9 – Bule Sky Studio. 9r – kaman985shu. 9l – elwynn. 11b – Orientaly. 11tl – freya-photgrapher. 12 – acinquantadue. 13tl, 13tr, 15tr, 17bm, 17br – Joe Gough. 13bl – Danny Smythe. 13br – Daniel Etzold. 13bm – 3445128471. 14tr – Cvijun. 14bm – Noraluca013. 15bm – Lyubov Kobyakova. 16 – OlegDoroshin. 17tr – Paul Brighton. 17br – Jacek Chabraszewski. 17tl – Pixelbliss. 18 – Robyn Mackenzie. 19 – GrigoryL. 20 – El Nariz. 21tl – khemawattana. 21tr – oksana2010. 21bl – Hong Vo. 21br – D. Pimborough. 22t – Gertan. 22b – Evgeny Karandaev. 23t – Velentina Proskurina. 23b – bestv.